Rita Watson has been a spiritual medium for thirty-two years. Through this time, she has been in contact with many people, not just through readings with the spirit world, but others who have needed her help when being haunted in their own personal space. She considers it as the most wonderful gift given to her and if taken away, part of her would go with it.

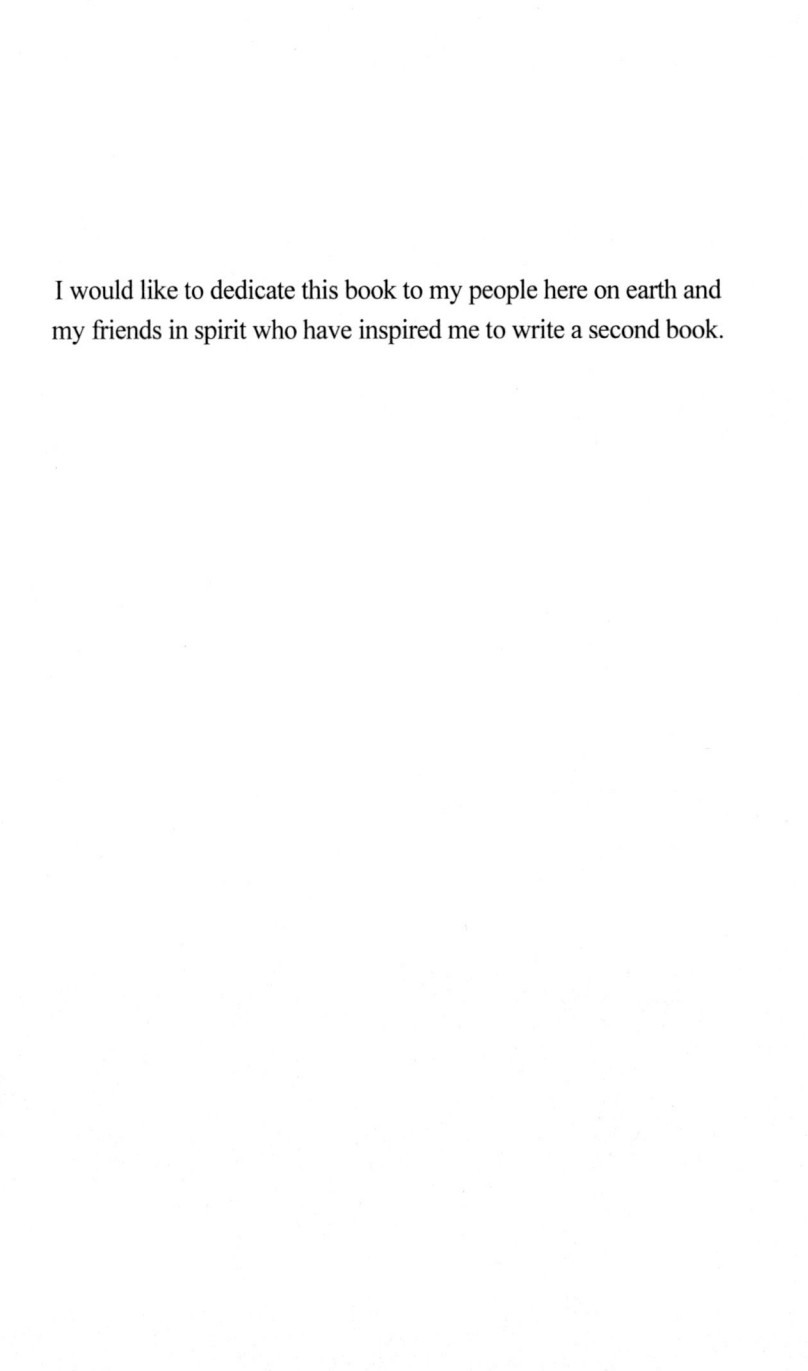

I would like to dedicate this book to my people here on earth and my friends in spirit who have inspired me to write a second book.

Rita Watson

RITA'S PEOPLE

AUSTIN MACAULEY PUBLISHERS™
LONDON • CAMBRIDGE • NEW YORK • SHARJAH

Copyright © Rita Watson 2022

The right of Rita Watson to be identified as author of this work has been asserted by the author in accordance with section 77 and 78 of the Copyright, Designs and Patents Act 1988.

All rights reserved. No part of this publication may be reproduced, stored in a retrieval system, or transmitted in any form or by any means, electronic, mechanical, photocopying, recording, or otherwise, without the prior permission of the publishers.

Any person who commits any unauthorised act in relation to this publication may be liable to criminal prosecution and civil claims for damages.

A CIP catalogue record for this title is available from the British Library.

ISBN 9781398461130 (Paperback)
ISBN 9781398461147 (ePub e-book)

www.austinmacauley.com

First Published 2022
Austin Macauley Publishers Ltd®
1 Canada Square
Canary Wharf
London
E14 5AA

I wish to thank all those people who have allowed me to write about their amazing spiritual readings and especially to say thank you to Claire and her son, James, as without their help, I would not have been able to get this book written.

Preface

I wrote my last autobiography of a modern-day medium and had it published in 1997. Since then, a whole lot has happened in my life, strange and unusual experiences have driven me to write again and share this with you. This gift that has been given to me from the depths of despair has shown me a new life and a new beginning.

In my first book, I spoke to you from my heart and soul, how in some way I conquered all, from losing my mum at the age of seven to being molested by foster parents, then thrust into the family my dad had made for me, where I was locked in the attic for hours on end.

Then at the age of eleven, going into a children's home where I was raped and torn by boys where I should have been in the care of that home, then by no fault of my own, I married a man who mentally and bodily abused me up to the age of forty. Where suddenly out of the blue, I was given a new lease of life, where I was able to leave the old behind and go forward with the new in the way of meeting John, my husband now, to which I cannot thank God enough, it saved me from a fate worse than death.

Then, unbelievable as it may be at the same time, this gift from the spirit world was given to me and there, in all its glory, stood the spirit world, where I could communicate with my dad and many more spirits. This opened my eyes and all the six senses, where I could suddenly see into the next world like opening a doorway and seeing the light. It came in a way of an outer body change and since then I have not looked back. When you have spiritual contact, a lot of things become clear, like why we suffer? Why sometimes life can be difficult? But we survive, and that is what living is all about.

I have called this book 'Rita's People' because we live on earth to nurture the soul, then we go into spirit to understand the working of the body and why we have to survive. So both the body and spirit are one, they are both people, the one in the body, then there is the soul which has to grow while we are here. I am here as a phone line between the two worlds, and to try and prove that we do live on beyond that which we call an overcoat, that we shred on our passing.

Chapter One

I awoke to find, sitting on my bed, a wonderful person full of love and light, there is no shadow as expected from the moonlight shining through the bedroom window. I suddenly feel weak and little knowing at that precise moment that this great person had been sent from the spirit world just for me, wrapping me in that warmth and security that only they can give, I am lifted up only to be told how lucky I am, as only a few people will see before death what I will be shown tonight.

As my spirit body approached the ceiling, I looked across to the windowsill in my room that was on the right and sitting quite plainly was a little man in a clown's suit, he was smiling and looked content and happy. My guide whom I realised by now was Ralfeta, my life guide, (when he was on the earth, he lived in a monastery, he was then a Tibetan monk, I often saw him in a brown cloak which covered his whole body, even his face seemed to be obscure sometimes.)

Ralfeta then told me the clown would keep an eye on things until I returned. I then relaxed and felt myself being carried further and further, there was a lightness around my body, it felt good, ecstatic even, as though the whole troubles of the world were falling away, a floatiness that I have never felt before, then I heard laughter, people talking, a cheerful atmosphere, like a party, is how you would describe it. People of all ages were coming up to me and saying, "Hello Rita, nice to see you." Funny, I thought, they know my name. Ralfeta had read my thoughts, he said, "They all know you because they are your family and friends that have passed into the spirit before you were born but, of course, you don't know them but you will one day."

My guide then took my hand, I waved goodbye to everybody, then suddenly, I was jerked down into a room. At first, it looked dark and I could not see anyone or anything, but as I got used to the atmosphere around me, I was overjoyed because sitting in her favourite chair in her sitting room, I saw Granny Harmer, we called her that when we were children because that is how it was then and I felt especially close to her. She was the gran that looked after us for a year as my father had gone off and left my younger sister and me in her care. At that moment, she was talking to me but I do not know to this day what my gran was saying, but I believe it was advice and sometimes, somewhere that advice has helped me in my life, she would have liked that.

Then, as abruptly as she came, she went. Ralfeta told me it was time to go with him, I then felt myself floating upwards again but this time, I was outside going around buildings, I do not know where it was but it had a feeling of being outside, then I looked down and I suddenly panicked as I had no body, then I was told by my guide, "of course, you will not have a body, you are in the spirit realms and here you leave your earthly body behind when you go home to the spirit world". I then seemed to drift into a child's bedroom Ralfeta said, "look at her," the child was tossing and turning, I noticed a doll by her side, she was very ill with a high temperature, Just by laying your hands and spiritual thoughts onto the young girl and you could cure her, as I did so, she stopped tossing and turning, turned over and went to sleep in a peaceful condition. Then, as if by magic, I was back in my own bed, I looked across to the clown still sitting on the windowsill. He waved to me and then disappeared. I then fell asleep but remembered every detail in the morning, which was marvellous. From this moment on, I knew things were going to be different, the communication got stronger from the spirit world.

The spirit side has a great sense of humour and harmony about them. Even if during their stay here on the earth plane, things had not gone well, they will still come back with a great feeling and strong well-being. Nicer things happen over there, an understanding, perhaps a little remorse, especially for those who have done wrong by others but they begin to note the whole story of the universe so to speak and this encourages them and they can survive death to return a better person, they find the bad part in their soul and put it right, this will then lead to wanting to return to make a fresh start in the earthbound world.

It can take up to anything from nine months to hundreds of years, depending on that soul. Each time we return, it has to be as a baby because we have to learn the evolvement of the earth all over again. We all have a right to be on this earth, it was given to us. I know we have rules set by the government, etc, but that is because of things we have had to learn in our past lives and of others. We have a duty to ourselves but nobody has the right to run our lives, we are born to prove who we are and why we are here? Whether we have money and life seems wonderful or if we do not have wealth, maybe poor, or living on the streets, we own part of this world of ours and that is what counts, so we must live our lives to the best of our ability, not by the rules that others think they should bestow upon us. Give and it will be given back to you. You will feel happy in doing so, you cannot beat that happiness, being happy inside shows on the outside, people around you will see this, it will shine through from your well-being even before they meet you.

If a person had been feeling down and they see you and they feel happy again, how good is that? Some people appear happy on the surface but deep inside they are suffering, it could be because of bereavement, sorrow in their lives, so help is at hand through a medium. To see a person go, feeling happier makes me feel good inside, that's all I ask, it's not hard, but it is hard when there is so much stress in our lives. I know I have been there and it can pull you down to the depths of despair if you let it, but if you try and put it aside just for a fleeting moment and draw spirit into your inner self, they will help. Just believe and they will be there beyond all doubt, that's what I did and now years later, I am a different person. I know I am happy, I put aside everything materialistic for happiness and it worked, the same as we all have, including jealousy, selfishness and greed, when we go into the spirit, if we can do this while we are here then the world will look different and you also can find that happiness. God wants you to be happy, so go out there and grab it.

My life now looks stabilised and I see a good future for me. Before, all I could see was a deep black hole and no way forward, but spirit work in a way that only they know how and guide you where you need to go, as I explained again in my last book how I have three guides, Ralfeta who is my life guide and has helped me a lot when I have been on the edge.

Then I have 'Chinho' who is Chinese and very knowledgeable, he has an insight into all that has been before and can see into the future for me, sometimes he can see years ahead, which can help a great deal when it comes to giving readings or sittings. I can read people because they are in desperate situations and need help to see if there is a future for them and other times, it can be just a sitting because we sit and wait for messages from our loved ones and this gives great comfort to those who need it. Chinho gives me the most precious thing in our lives and that is the knowledge of the here and now, the future for us.

Then there is my Red Indian, he brings in a lot of healing for the mind as well as the body, this healing is strong and can be sent through the mind as well as the body. It is done with the hands, you can feel the heat as it penetrates through the person who is asking for it. This guide has not given me his name, I am still waiting for it, he believed in life after death in all his earthly life. He is so happy to be there helping people now that he is on the other side, he says he feels very privileged, he tells me that when he went over, he was able to learn of greater things in his spiritual being and that road has lead him to me, for which I am very grateful especially in the early years of being a medium, where I needed to sort out a lot of experiences in my head and he was there to do it.

These three men are here to help me in all that I do through the spirit world, I feel very lucky in a way to be able to experience this in my lifetime on earth, the only other guide I know that has passed through me is, Alice. I was given Alice at a church meeting one year from another medium, she is able to help me while I work on the platform doing the church services, she is a great help in showing me who I am to go to in the audience by putting a light over their head to show me the way. I did learn a lot from her and she gave me plenty of encouragement when I needed it, which was loads in the early days because it's not easy getting up in front of people with nothing but your soul to offer.

I did get negative at one of the last meetings I attended, it was at the church in Laindon Essex on starting my clairvoyance at the end of the service. I had trouble communicating with the audience; it seemed to be going pear-shaped, so in the end, I had to give up, said I was sorry to everyone but nothing was happening, I just sat down and if the floor could have opened up and swallowed me, it would have been a good thing but nothing was that simple. I felt humiliated and embarrassed and could not get out of the church fast enough but that was years ago, I have learned a lot since then, although that experience changed my pathway forever. I have done small communities since but I have not wanted to go back to working in the church Rostrums since obviously it was not meant to be.

Time is man-made and if we think time is flying by, we have made it happen ourselves by fitting too much into it, we try to conquer everything but we cannot do this, we are only mere mortals and as hard as we think we are coping, life has a strange way of deceiving us, I count myself in on this as I do try to fit too much all the time. When we pass into the spiritual realms, there is no going back to a time before limiting ourselves, we have to learn a new way to go forward and of managing our souls in a new way. This evolves slowly, that is why sometimes it takes years before we can communicate with our loved ones in the material world and other times if we have already had the knowledge they can come through very quickly.

After realising that being a medium can be a rewarding experience, it became obvious to me that there was to be a change in my life, that change at first was materialistic we had the opportunity to buy a little house opposite the launderette, the launderette was given back to me by my ex-husband, he had let it go to rack and ruin and when I took it back over again in 1992, it took a lot of hard work and effort to rebuild it, of course, I could not have managed without the help of John, my husband now, so all my spiritual work was put on hold for a while as I concentrated building up the business. In two years, all the hard work paid off and we had managed to save up so we could go on holiday. On discussing where we would like to go, we both decided that we would like to go to Egypt. John's mum and dad said they would look after the business and as it was summer, the shop was not so busy in the hot months, it seemed perfect. It is now 1994 and as I looked forward to going to Egypt; I had great expectations as the Egyptians are a very spiritual race and I had this feeling deep down that I was going to gain something from this holiday but at that moment, I did not realise how much it really was going to mean to me, as I mentioned in my last book, I had experienced before on other holidays but none of these had prepared me for what happened in Egypt that year.

On arriving at our destination, we were disappointed with the hotel, it was right in the middle of Luxor, dusty, dirty, and the room was very small but this was not going to deter me from enjoying the wonders of the world and what it might hold for me, that first evening as we sat up on the roof of the hotel, a warm breeze blew across from the desert where you could see the Valley of the Kings in all its glory, it was like a hairdryer, peaceful, tranquil with a lot to offer, I felt.

The next day, as we gathered in the lounge to see what excursions we could go on, I felt the excitement of something but could not put my finger on it. We had at this point decided to go on an excursion of two days up the river Nile. John and I both loved boats and water so this seemed a great idea, unknown to me at that time, although I felt something, it seemed like a great adventure and what happened has stayed with me forever. That is why I want to share it with you. The boat was to take us up the river to Aswan. On the way, we stopped at many temples; they were very interesting, each one had its own story to tell and I felt we did learn a lot.

That was until this particular temple we stopped at, which had a different approach to it, as we got off the boat we had to make our way to horses and carts on the quayside as the temple lay in the land and it would be a long way to walk so this transport was laid on for us. It was hot, the streets were dusty with strange smells. I remember saying to John, "I do not think I would like to be stranded here", little did I know that these words would come back to haunt me.

We got to the temple, which was huge, much bigger than any of the others, the ship's crew had told us to take the number on the side of the cart and that one would return for us to get back to the boat, as we approached the temple, an amazing thing happened to me, I stood there transfixed because as I looked, the scenery changed and in its place was a scene from the twelfth century, everything looked different. A wonderful feeling came over me, I could not move and I felt Jesus Christ was there giving his blessing and then as suddenly it had come it went and we were back in modern times and I could walk again, I seemed to have been in a trance of some sort, after looking around for a little longer we then went back to the stop-off point but the horse and cart were nowhere to be seen. We waited and waited then panic set in, it was nearly ten o'clock, time for the boat to leave, we could hear the whistle in the background telling everybody to return, I was beginning to wonder if we would be stranded in this strange place, we did not had to worry though, they sent somebody out to look for us and we got back safely but the experience I had at the temple that day changed me, I think I found God within myself.

This is not the only thing that happened to me while in Egypt, on taking another day out to the Valley of the Kings and Queens tombs, all these have been discovered through special digs by the government and since they found king Tut's tomb everything has got to be documented. On this day, we went and as we were coming back, we had to go through a marketplace where the Egyptians were selling their wares, when suddenly, before me the whole place opened up and I was seeing another tomb being found, I told John what I had seen, he smiled as if to say 'okay' and we left it at that. Egypt had stood up to its reputation, spiritual, mystical, especially Cairo and its eighteen million people. The museum, the pyramids, camels and of course the heat, oh the heat, especially in august but it was amazing.

Just going ahead a little to nineteen ninety-seven to finish this story, John decided to turn the television onto BBC TWO as there was a documentary on Egypt. I could not believe what I was seeing and hearing, apparently, in the same spot that I had mentioned those words 'they are going to find another tomb soon' they had to move one of the market stalls to get to it but they had found a doorway to one of the biggest tombs ever uncovered, it had fifty rooms one for each of the king's son's. This king unknown at that time must have had a long life or lots of wives, it was marvellous to think that I knew it was there three years before anyone else did, so I feel Egypt played a big part in my life and I hope one day to return.

I feel peace and tranquillity around me, perhaps a little apprehensive but the wonder of what is to come. This is the feeling I feel when I am waiting to do a sitting, waiting for that person to come through the door to give them that feed of knowledge, which is beyond this world and that our loved ones that have gone before are not very far away. We live with reason and understanding and sometimes this can be our downfall, especially when we have lost someone close and everything that we are living for has gone out the window. I feel that I have to tell you this because we are in a world of modern technology and sometimes we forget that our loved ones are there looking after us until of course, that person walks through the door and we find a way beyond all our reasoning that the information I give them is definitely from their loved ones and they are in disbelief at times of what is told to them. Some sitters, however much they believe, they are a little bit scared and I hope when they leave me, they are laughing and feeling relieved and in a way that they are then able to carry on with their everyday lives. This is what a sitting is all about. I call mine a sitting rather than a reading as I explained before and hopefully I can give them information and they are in no doubt that it has come from their loved ones in spirit.

The younger generation is becoming more aware of spiritualism, they always need to know more so as well as giving them the special words from their loved ones, who have gone before they are also getting a lot of help with the modern problems of today, which affect their lives deeply and by doing this the spirits are giving them back their lives and the courage to carry on so, therefore, the help that we get from beyond the grave is so precious to us all, this has become very obvious within the last year or so. I have noticed a large change in what I am being given from the spirit world for the younger sitters, it seems they want to know more of what is happening to them and what the future holds in store for the years ahead. I am not, for one minute, saying I am a fortune-teller as they are a different class altogether but quite often, I help the sitters over a bad time in their life and when it's all over and they are out the other side, smiling it is all worthwhile.

Below is part of a letter which I received from Kate. Kate was by chance there at the right time to help, it was while I was searching for a publisher for my first book and Kate was on the other end of the line, from there she came on a sitting and for the advice that she got from the spirit world, her loved ones helped gave her the determination and strength to do what changed her life and made it better, the letter goes:

"Dear Rita, I would like to thank you for your help and support over the last couple of months. I am now back with my parents looking forward to a more fulfilling new year, thank you. I am sure I will see you in the new year just to see how or where my path is going. Take care till then, Kate."

When I receive letters like these, it is payment enough to know spirits have helped. In years to come, everybody will be able to communicate with our loved ones in spirit and soon it will be shown. Psychometry can play a great part in our spiritual communications as sometimes people can hold a loved one close to them and I find it hard to hear what they are saying but by holding a personal item that either belonged to that person or a photograph, it can bring to life something from the past and when the sitter will recognise what you are saying, suddenly, the tears will flow and from that moment their loved ones can communicate much more easily and it makes for a wonderful sitting. I have had many people come to me out of the blue, especially while I had the launderette because it brings you in touch with so many people from all walks of life, people, my people of spirit and earth.

Chapter Two

I said in my first chapter that I had taken over the launderette from my ex-husband, Norman. This was a great asset to me as I could reach out to ordinary people with the gift I have been given. This is why I believe spirit opened the way for me to work hard but I enjoyed every minute of it.

I wrote to a magazine called Eva, about how I became a medium and the story behind it. They decided to print it because they had just started to write about unusual psychic abilities, in fact, they were one of the first. Since that time fifteen years ago, a whole host of magazines have taken up this challenge, which is good because it seems more and more people are becoming involved and seeing that this life is not the end but just the beginning. At that time, I wrote to Eva explaining the situation I had been in and how the spirit world had reached out and helped me, I had a wonderful picture of myself and Tammy, our German shepherd dog, she sadly passed on in the year 2000 but of course, she is always here with me in spirit. It basically outlined how my father-in-law, Eddie, came to me and gave his approval of what I am doing, helping people with spirit contact. At that time, he had been passed for over seven years, this made me believe he had Tammy with him, the thing he always used to do, when he was alive, was to tickle me in the ribs and that is what I felt then and I believe he did it to let me know he was there. It was a weird feeling, perhaps a new experience for me at the same time it was wonderful because the full knowledge was creeping up on me day by day, yes there is life after we die and from that time there is no going back, only forward and that was twenty years ago but it still feels like yesterday.

Eddie helped me overcome a lot of obstacles and one of them being the control my ex-husband had over me, even though it was his own son, and lots of things besides this, I must say, he was there for me in abundance. My ex has blamed me even now for the breakup of our marriage, after all the suffering I had in my life with him but it was Norman who had all the affairs and whose girlfriend blasted me with phone calls year after year, for six whole years to be precise. He went back to her three times, we lost our house in Essex because of her and I had to go begging to the council offices to find us somewhere to live because the mortgage had not been paid with all that strain, everything, I am afraid the trust in our marriage had gone, so when I met John he was to change my life into what I have today. Basically, Eva magazine outlined all of that to which a marvellous thing happened. From that story, a local newspaper 'Yellow Advertiser' got hold of the story of me writing my first book and they came and wrote a piece on me and it all came out and as I was working in the launderette at that time, I became quite well known.

Just after it was printed in the paper, a man came into the launderette, he was at that time a heavy drinker, smelt terrible, it was obvious that he did not care for his welfare. He came up to me and said, "I read your story in the local paper and have pinned it up on the wall."

Laughing, I said, "What? Are you going to do throw darts at it or something?"

He then came back very serious and said, "No, I just want you to know that if you can survive all that and get through it, then I can do it as well." Those words had never left me as I carried on over the next few months. One day Bob (I will call him that) popped into the launderette. I was surprised to see him and as I looked, he was a changed man. He had changed from a sad drink-fuelled oldish man into a younger version of himself, he had stopped drinking and began to wash and look after himself and over the next couple of years decided it was time to help others in the same situation that he had been in. Now that my people out there, as I said, I will never forget that one person I helped and then he went out to help so many. How good is that, even to this day I see Bob out and about and though I am not in the launderette anymore, he always stops by for a chat. Well, I do marvel at what spirit manage to achieve and I do know if it was not for the spirit, I would not have written my first book, let alone this one. It could have well been a different story for Bob and the many he helped now and possibly more in the future, things do happen in mysterious ways.

Going back a little, I was back in the launderette and one day a lady by the name of Sue came rushing in, she was in a flap as most people are whose washing machine has broken down, she had a few choice words to say about her poor washing machine, which I cannot repeat she said, "Only had it for a few months. Well, looks like you will be seeing a lot more of me as it cannot be repaired for a couple of weeks," but the spirit had other ideas, it was not a couple of weeks as it turned out more like a couple of months because unknown to me, Sue was being lined up for a reading, apparently, something unusual was going on in her life and the full picture of it all came out from her loved ones in spirit through me. We decided of all places to have the reading at the back of the launderette, funny you might think as it was a spur-of-the-moment decision, one I call a reading but it was convenient for us both. Sue was happy about that and so was I, the miracle of what was to come through will stay with me forever, I have to share this with you, my people out there, it could be unbelievable but what happened hand on heart, was true, as I said, Sue's machine had broken down and she was one of these people you could get on with and chat, of course, it came round to me being a medium thus her having the reading. There were, of course, personal things said that actually led in the end, to a remarkable story and wonderful ending, I would not print some of this, of course, but as the reading progressed the whole story of her brother came out. I will call him Derek to give the family personal protection and confidence to let me print this. Derek had gone out to America on a business trip, while out there, he met up with a despicable person and that involvement led to a shooting and a person being killed, I saw the gun, the person and also Derek in jail, at that time, he had been there for quite a while and apparently on Death Row. The poor man had not pulled the trigger but had been in the wrong place at the wrong time, so here he was, miles from home and not knowing if he was going to see his family and friends again. Well, Sue could not believe it, but as I tuned in the spirit world, I kept repeating that he would be coming home and they would be seeing him again, Sue seemed to pick

26

up at this but as soon as she felt positive she seemed to feel down again she said, "He could not see it happening, I just cannot see it happening." Even when I told her there was a cross, a clergyman that visited him in prison had become a friend to Derek, Sue agreed that it was right what I was being told. After the reading, I did see Sue on and off, still lugging in the washing, I did mention to her that surely it would be cheaper to get another washing machine and we laughed about it but I still think she needed that link with me, at that time, hoping perhaps to hear more but no more was said. Then after about six months of not seeing her, she suddenly appeared again and to my amazement, she sort of shouted it from the rooftop, "Rita, its good news but also some bad news, Derek was coming home that was the good news but the reason for this was he had had a heart attack and needed surgery so he was allowed to come home for the treatment and was able to stay now in England," so you see the family did see him again not obviously in the best of circumstances but a great relief was had by all, especially me, I do trust what spirit tells me but sometimes it takes longer than you think.

During my nine years at the launderette, things happened so often out of the blue, I do not believe in giving out bad news from the spirit world because the news I give should be enlightenment. The sitters should go away from the reading, happy with the knowledge that their loved ones are there for them but that time things were a little different, I will call this young lady, Jane, the evidence that was given to her from the spirit world was to help her more than one can say. The reading that day started really well with a lot of good things for herself but then a change was in the air, especially when it came to her boyfriend at that time, drugs were mentioned, something that was connected to him as well as a circle of friends that he was involved in, Jane said drugs were a no with her boyfriend so I felt it was more to do with the friends he was with, then I heard an almighty thud it was like somebody was being murdered, I was not told how, who, but I saw a knife in that group of friends, as I tuned in further, I pointed out it was not him being killed, the spirit said they were sorry but this was going to happen before Christmas, it was now August. Also, they gave the information that would help her when she needed it and then we ended the reading because simply it was mind-blowing, we both could not quite take it all in at the time but I know spirit is always right. Jane was a bit bewildered but who would not be given the information she had just been given but she did take it all in her stride, it felt very hot in the room but after we relaxed and cooled down with cool drinks, things came back to normal. In December, the same year I was very busy in the Launderette, everybody was preparing to get their last things laundered before Christmas, it was buzzing, excitement in the air and that was just the adults. The children, well, you know how they are, usually on a fast-forward button I would say, when all of a sudden, Jane was there in front of me with tears and disbelief in her eyes. As I calmed her down and could get a word out of her the whole story came tumbling out, she told me that it was her boyfriend using the drugs but she assured me that she certainly did not know this, at the time of the reading, looking at her I believed her, apparently, he and his friends had gone to a nightclub in Ilford and somehow got into an argument with the doorman and stabbed him twelve times and killed him, he was now being held awaiting trial but one good thing Jane assured me that the reading she had in the summer helped her a lot to cope with the ordeal. The last time I saw Jane was March/April, a time when she came in to see me, she told me she had had enough and wanted to end the relationship, who could blame her? She had been through a lot, at least she gave it her best, what happened after that I do not know, although, she still was very worried about ending the relationship as she said he had people on the outside that might harm her. Let's hope her life changes for the best.

This is one example of what spirit can achieve. Not all my spirit encounters are based on readings. This is an account of what happened to Maureen when she came to me for help.

An account of Maureen's Paranormal Experience

About a year ago, Maureen moved into a new house. This is her story:

My husband and I sensed a presence as if there was a third-person living with us, every weekend our grandson, Kieran, who was two and a half years old, came to stay with us. Regularly at about two o'clock in the morning, Kieran would call out to us to come to his room, each time it was the same story, he would say that a man and his mummy were sitting at the foot of the bed, he explained how the mummy was smiling and the man seemed to be clearing his throat, however, Kieran was not frightened at this because he was a nice man. Whilst speaking to a neighbour, I was told that Kieran was referring to the previous occupants and that the man had died quite recently. I was troubled by this news, in view of the fact that Kieran was waking up every night when he stayed with us.

After discussing it with my husband, we decided to call on outside help. We elected to invite Rita, who has some experience in this kind of situation, to come around one afternoon. Rita went upstairs and entered all the bedrooms, it was in Kieran's bedroom that she announced that she felt a presence. We sat downstairs whilst Rita remained in Kieran's room and communed with whoever it was, she asked him why he was still here and what he wanted, he replied that he meant no harm and that he was looking after Kieran, he went on to say that in his previous life he had a child who had tragically died, he then told Rita he was sorry and would leave. Since that time, Kieran has only referred once to this episode, asking where the nice man had gone. It is only my husband now that feels there is something extraordinary about the house.

I have written this down to the exact word that Maureen gave to me, since then she has moved, let's hope the new house is clear of spirit or her husband who I suspect is very open to the world beyond this one or he will be at it again. A child will only say what he or she sees as with any young person, they will only say what they see or sense it cannot be made up, so the truth is out there. What Kieran saw at two and a half can only be the truth, it is there for us all to see.

I met Lisa just after a friend of hers drowned in a boating lake near where we lived, his name was Jay, although they called him JJ and his family belonged to the funfair, they had land where they used to stay during the winter months, not far from the Launderette as it happens, JJ was a great friend of Lisa's and she missed him so much. He was only eighteen when he passed, she said it felt like her world had come to an end but funnily enough, two weeks after he had died, he came to Lisa and she was scared out of her wits (her words) this is where I came in. Lisa came to see me stricken with grief, she wanted me to go to her house, as from when she was a little girl she had felt spirits around her. With JJ this was different though, it was someone she cared about. Actually, when I finally got around to her house, it was not JJ I picked up but a woman, as I tuned in, Lisa shouted 'I can see her, I can see her', as soon as the spirit appeared she went so I was unable to communicate to see who it was, Lisa said I should not have done that. Then an uncle of JJ appeared, as he did so, the woman who was there before told Lisa she would come to terms with JJ's death although she feels emotional now, everything is for a reason. I think Lisa felt happier after that.

On my way back to my house, which was within walking distance, JJ was suddenly at my side, in fact, he nearly tripped me up as we walked, he came around in front of me, he never said anything but his action spoke louder than words because when I told Lisa this she was amazed, JJ would do that to her when he was here in our world. I feel Lisa should take up spirit work as she was very strong but we have free will and if she ever wanted to, the spirit world would be waiting. In fact, she said once that I was her role model, Lisa then said she was not scared of dying anymore and to her, it is a beautiful and wonderful place we all go to, and well my guess is she is right about that, but a role model? Me? Not so sure.

While the Launderette kept me busy, my mediumship seemed to strengthen but sometimes it all got too much. I do have little things in the shape of poems sent my way, which inspires me to carry on. Like this one:

Have you ever felt, you would like to know, just what the future holds, Is it sadness or happiness, which perhaps tomorrow holds? Good luck or perhaps a meeting, that soon could change your way, for the future's here, to paint its story, in all, its given ways. So book now with Rita, to help you find your way, in the map of life that happens to change, every single day.

I had the Launderette given back to me by my ex-husband. I built it up with the help of John to the profitable business it is today. In nineteen ninety-two, not only did we take on the shop but we decided to also buy a small house opposite, which actually put us on the property ladder. Just after buying the house, John decided to change his job and instead of being a resident caretaker in the senior school where we lived, he decided to go to a junior school, which was non-resident, giving us the chance to move into our own house. It was lovely to be on our own property and we settled in, it was while John was at this next school that a funny thing happened. It was while I was closing up the shop, cleaning down the machines at the end of the day, when John walked in but as he did so, a spirit man was right behind him, the spirit seemed really worried about something. I asked him who he was and why was he following John, he replied, "Tell him he has forgotten to lock the door of one of the buildings." he said he was one of the old caretakers and he was keeping an eye on the school. When I mentioned this to John, he said, "Oh dear, I have forgotten to lock the dining-room door." it was an outside door so it was very important, as he dashed out back to the school, I thanked the spirit man, he never told me his name but I knew he had lived on the site of the school at one time. He had passed over, of course, but I should imagine he is still there to this day looking after the school.

Just before I left the Launderette for good, I have to tell you this remarkable story. One day, as I was cleaning out the bottom of the dryers, it was by chance I found a heavy gold man's wedding ring, I said by chance because usually you scoop up all the dust and throw it into a black bag but it was there, shining in the dirt. I cleaned the ring up and put it in the drawer and forgot all about it. Over the next couple of years, there it stayed until one day, I was talking to a lady who was doing her washing and was discussing the Launderette and how I was needing another girl to help me out in the evenings, she then said her teenage daughter was looking for something to earn a little cash, I said to send her along and we can have a chat. Anyway, we did and Donna started working for me. One day, somebody asked Donna if she had found some keys and perhaps had them in the drawers as she opened the drawer, she could not believe her eyes, there sitting in the drawer, was her Dad's ring, the one I had found a couple of years before, of course. She was over the moon to get it back but we do wonder at what wonderful things can happen, I am sure their loved ones in spirit had a hand there so she could get it back, you just cannot make up these things that happen out of the blue.

I have now left the launderette. I decided it was time to sell up and move on, I was now finding it harder to keep it going 24/7. I have been very grateful for the nine years I had there, building it up to the profitable business it is today, from when my ex-husband, Norman left it to me in a terrible state, so as I stand there, I admire the work John and I had put into it. I had met loads of lovely people along the way so now as I close my eyes and turn my back and leave it in the capable hands of Alison, who bought the whole lot from me and she is still there to this day. John at first worked with a car firm RT Rates, then he moved on to buy a cafe in West cliff – on the sea near the south end of Essex. I then decided to help him out in the café, while feeling this would be a chance to meet more people so I could carry on with doing more readings.

During that time, I met Roy Marsden, he was first seen on TV years ago in a detective series. He had, at that time, decided to take over the old Royal Theatre in West cliff, which was just over the road from the café. He said he was trying to do something with it and bring life back to a run-down place. He told me he had it for five years. We became friends and during this friendship, I actually gave him a reading amongst other things personal to himself, his grandmother mentioned to me about a farmhouse, to which he told me was correct as he was just in the middle of buying one, well I said, she has shown me feathers everywhere. Roy told me he did not know what it meant but he would be going to see the farm next week and he would let me know if anything crops up. When I next saw him, he was ecstatic because when they reached the farm and went inside a bird had got inside the chimney and it must have panicked as there were feathers everywhere, this is what his grandmother was trying to tell him, how remarkable was that? After that, Roy was a valuable customer to us in the cafe as he brought a lot more people with him from the theatre, the actors that were in the play that he was producing at the time. So to say it lightly, they were all very interested in my gift of mediumship as I talked to them about it a lot. One night, John and I were invited over to the theatre to watch the play they were producing, but halfway through, I suddenly saw a character in black, cross the stage and go through one of the actors. I told Roy the next day, he obviously could not understand it but two days later, there was an argument between that certain actor and another, which led him to walk out, it did resolve itself but I am sure this strange man in black had caused it, a wandering spirit from past days, no doubt.

John and I are gipsies at heart as we always have the need to move on after a while. This is what happened in May 1997. We bought a new house not far from the Launderette, it did us well and I loved it as it was something given to us from all the hard work we had done. The cafe John had bought was about twenty miles away, which meant a thirty-minute drive but you do it and at the time think nothing of it.

It was this year also that my son Dean got married to Sarah. I had mentioned at some point that he would meet someone and she would steal his heart and she did, as Sarah was his first and only girlfriend and they were made for each other. Anyway, a month after they were married, disaster struck for the royal family because on August 31 1997, Princess Diana got killed in a car crash, at that time mourning of everyday people was paramount but for me, something remarkable happened. A couple of days after this tragic event, I awoke to find standing next to me in my bedroom, Princess Diana herself and as things unfolded in that first week, it will be with me for the rest of my life.

I felt honoured that she had chosen me as her channel because she could have chosen any medium, I guess it was all prepared even before she passed that I was the one chosen for her to appear to, was it because I read the Sun newspaper? Her favourite, I do not know and I really cannot explain. On the Tuesday of the first week, Diana told me we were going to hear of another death and then on Wednesday, September 3, we heard of the death of mother Teresa. I was stunned, she was so close to Diana, I believe it was meant to be they had each other in the next world. Then the next day, I heard from Diana again, this time she told me two things would come to light, one was that DODI had bought her a ring and she had been planning to marry him. The next day, in the Sun it appeared as headline news. The next night, she told me in a dream about a secret garden where she used to go to as a child and then again the next day it appeared in the Sun newspaper that she was going to be buried on an island at her childhood home, it was in the middle of a lake there. On Friday, before her funeral, she came to me with her father, I knew it was him because, at the precise time, I was reading about her in the Sun and all of a sudden, my leg went completely numb. I believe to this day it was her father standing with her because he had a poorly leg in his last days and it was his way of telling me he was there. I often get these things and using one of my six senses is what I say and it was proof that Diana was with him. Then that night, I had a vision; I saw a celebration as I could see champagne glasses and I realised later she was telling me that this was the year of the Queen and Prince Philip golden wedding anniversary, which actually took place on November the same year, but then Diana told me it would only be for another twelve years as in the year 2009, something would happen to change things, she did not tell me anymore. For another four weeks, I did not hear any more and I thought that was it but out of the blue, I had a vision of Diana on a beautiful golden beach as I looked, I could see on the side stone steps but I heard her say to me, "Do not go up there it is dangerous", then I realised she was talking to a young girl who was standing there with her, I could feel the warm sandy beach beneath my feet, the water on my right was clear and blue. Princess Diana then held the girl's hand, she looked about twelve years old. On the same beach was a small white van, which looked like it was selling fish, they both looked excited and relaxed together as though they knew each other. As the picture started to fade, I saw buildings at the top of the jagged rocks but to get to them, you had to walk the long way round, I felt Diana was telling me you cannot take a shortcut around anything, the very next day, sure enough there it was in the paper once again, in fact, it covered the centre pages of the Sun about a young girl who Diana had made friends with while she was on holiday in the Bahamas, I never cease to be amazed. Then straight after that the very next night, I had a vision of what looked like a porcelain doll, behind her was a beautiful blue dress, then a week later, it appeared in The News of the World about a porcelain doll they were selling of Diana in a blue dress, how great was that.

In those weeks, it was an honour to be her spiritual gateway. On November 25 1997, I was sitting reading the beautiful stories of Diana and the people she loved, when all of a sudden I had a blackout, a picture emerged, I was in a car crash, I could not move my arms or legs, not even open my eyes, let alone talk, but I could hear everything going on around me. I tried and tried to communicate but I could not. Suddenly, in my mind, I tried to reach for my phone but obviously, I could not, then I heard the sound of a pop bike going past, I thought blimey that is on the wrong side of the road for France, then there was silence, blackness again Diana was showing me her last moments in the car. I believe now, nearly ten years on, she was trying to tell me it was an awful accident, I believe it was.

My very last communication with Diana was December 1997, when she told me how proud she was of her boys, I saw a hall full of people and Harry receiving an award for history, whether this happened I do not know but I hope so, in the same vision, she showed me a young boy who was crippled. He told her that one day, he was going to run as fast as Linford Christie, well I felt at that precise moment that young boy was possibly going to join Diana soon. All I have written here in my book is true to what happened, as I said, why did she choose me, I do not know but I am glad she did because I can share my experience with all of you. I am sure she would like to know that she will be beside her boys forever because they were her life and always will be.

My dream would be to see the world at peace, for people not to suffer anymore, food for all and plenty of love to go around, to see flowers everywhere, and to see children's faces smiling as they do in spirit. My dream is to be able to help as many people as I can to understand that we do not die, we live on to see the sad faces smile again and to know that I have been able to do that with the help of spirit, I do hope my dream becomes reality.

Anyway, getting back to the cafe as we are still there, this is where I met Derek, as well as a lot of other people. Derek or Del Boy, as I used to call him as he reminded me of David Jason but he was very knowledgeable in ways of spirit. He had written a wonderful play and was at that time, trying hard to break into the business but without success, I tried hard to help him and I felt in many ways I did but not what he had hoped for. He had great potential but his work stopped him from fulfilling his dream, like many of us but he wrote lovely poetry and some he wrote for me. Over breakfast every morning this went on, I was touched by his thoughtfulness and this was a favourite of mine:

> An inspirational Man
> Inspired by everything he sees
> Written in the words of thee
> To find language in a rhyme
> Perpetrating hearts and minds
> People try to explain
> Perhaps just why?
> Many understandings tried
> He who can or so think he knows
> Rack their brains on countless goals
> Cleverly, the words unfolded
> Just like history, as they have told it
> In the plays that bring much pleasure
> In the name that is forever treasured
> One thing I now can see
> That to like him
> I will try to be
> Who knows, perhaps one day I will too
> Be thought about
> As we have you.

A first thought when reading this is, what is it all about? But you have to read it a few times before you understand the meaning of it, I am sure that this was Del boy's aim in life anyway, as far as I know, today he is still writing his words and perhaps helping others. We all parted our ways, when the lease of the cafe came to an end, we both decided not to take on the lease again but we did sell it, at a loss but sometimes the experience is lessons to be learned. It is a shame really but certain things never last but the memories are still there and I hope I have left a few good things for people to remember.

It is now the year 2000, the turn of the century, John decided as we did not have any commitments, we could go to Barcelona in Spain but all the time we were out there, I felt ill, which is unlike me. I put it down to a flu bug, I just could not shift it, in fact, I did not enjoy it one bit, I tried but the way I felt it was hopeless, it seemed endless that week and I was glad to return home. This year, in the beginning, was heartbreaking, we lost our dog, Tammy, it was February, she had massive tumours and I am afraid we had to let her go. It does not matter how often and how much you try to tell others that their animals are in spirit and they are alright, it still hurts so bad, we cried but as I said in my first book that animals do not realise they have passed over and one world leads into the other so they are still with you, although their spirits have left and their overcoat body been removed. Tammy played a special part in my life as when I had my story printed in Eva Magazine, she was there with me, playing her part on the front page with me. I wrote to the magazine telling my story of how I became a Medium, I was reborn at the age of forty when I met John and my life changed for the better, I thought again if I can do it, anybody out there can, as proved before with the gentleman that came into the Launderette a few years earlier, although as the year started with bad things within my career. Life changed as now we were not tied to the business, John had bought a large van and was working for a company delivering parcels and seemed at that time, he enjoyed that. I was at that time looking for a small job to keep me ticking over and that is when I bumped into Patricia, a friend of mine. We had been friends since we worked together in 1989 as cleaners in a school. Patricia had now become a supervisor in a college complex and asked if I would like to have a cleaning job with her and as it was only yards away from our house, I jumped at the chance.

Two main things happened to me after starting that job, one, I met Pamela, who was a teacher at the college and two, I found my long-lost friend Eileen again by bumping into her daughter, Joanne while shopping with John in Basildon. Joanne told me Eileen, being Joanne's mother, had cancer of the breast and was about to go into the hospital for an operation. Eileen and I go back years when our children were small but her family were close friends with Norman, my ex-husbands family so when we broke up, due to his infidelity, we lost touch and that bond we had as friends was lost because of it but somehow this meeting with Joanne was meant to be and it bought us back together again.

Joanne told me she had lost her dad, Cliff, to the spirit world and I am sure it was him, who bought us back together so here it was this unexpected meeting and on hearing about Eileen, this was a shock and I wanted to see her, Joanne thought it would be okay, I went to see her at her home, also when she went into the hospital. I took her a poem in a frame called footsteps in the sand. I am sure all you lovely people out there know this poem, it gives you a huge lift in times of need, Eileen loved it. After the operation, she had to go to Southend Hospital every day for six weeks to have radiotherapy as I was free during the day after doing my cleaning job early morning at college, I offered to take her each day, she was very grateful as the hospital was twenty miles away. I was happy I was able to take her also, we got back on track with our friendship, we were able, in the time we had together and it was like all those lost years floated away. We still keep our friendship to this day, sometimes you marvel at what our spirit friends will do.

Ongoing back to the workplace, my first book played a big part in getting in touch with the spirit realm, it was a way of introducing myself as a medium and when people read it, they quite often want a reading. This is how Pamela (the Teacher) got involved with me. When people read the book like her, the spirit starts to work through me. Pam was going through a bad and upsetting time with her current boyfriend, I felt she did not understand herself, let alone the relationship she was in. I told her that this person was not for her and she would be meeting someone else through her dancing, of course, she did not believe me, she felt a failure in that department and she said she would never meet the right person. I assured her she would, spirits are saying you just wait and see. Over the coming year, she dated others but they came to nothing, I kept saying to her to be patient during which she had another reading with me. There were other problems with her brother who was drinking heavily, I asked if her brother would come and see me as I had a message from their mother for him. She told me she wanted to have a word with him and sort things out once and for all, about what the mother meant, I was not sure. The meeting was arranged at my house. Peter (Pam's brother) came with an unexpected nervousness, he did not know what to expect, to be fair, nor did I, I put him at ease straight away by giving him some healing. I asked Pamela to stay because I felt she needed to hear what was going to be said. The healing went well, then all of a sudden a booming voice came through, "you either give up the drink or you will die", it took us all by surprise, then a lot of good things came through for Peter and I knew when he left that day a change would occur. Months later, he looked like a different man. After the reading, he went to AA and it had worked wonders, he had started writing a book not on alcoholism or anything like that but on the history of Ingatestone, where Pamela lived. It was really good and well thought out, I believe it was Peter's way of dealing with the drink and it got it out of his system. The same as myself with my first book, when I sat in the circle for the first time, they told us all who were there that the only way to sort out the past was to write about it, get it all down on paper and that is how I became to write my book, "Autobiography of a modern-day medium", in the first place, oh yes it helped, it was a great experience, it sorted a lot of things out in my head so I could finally go forward. Pamela became a good friend and as we worked in the same place. I often saw her, she also was a good friend of Patricia with some people you just click, don't you? So the three of us went out occasionally on birthdays, Christmas, etc. It was about two years in, on the job at the college and during that time there were many changes in Pamela's life as the time was changing for me, I was being directed for changes, Pam did eventually meet the man of her life, he was younger than her and he had a daughter, before family seemed a problem for her as I kept saying to Pam that when you meet people later in life, they have lived a large part of their life and it usually means that there is always family involved, I felt she did not quite understand what I meant but never mind, she thought this was different, she seemed to come to terms that this was different as she thought a lot of this man and she was able to share him with his daughter and lo-and-behold he could dance, she told me he was a wonderful dancing partner for her and yes, I did think that this man may be the one, time will tell as they say.

After that, I had to move on but we did meet again for the most marvellous birthday I had ever had, my son Richard had not spoken to me for fourteen years because I left the marital home due to his father's adultery but Richard could not forgive me the first six years. I was at my wit's end trying to come to terms with him being out of my life but suddenly on my 55 birthday, I had a letter from him wanting to meet up that is why I was over the moon on this special day and I was ready to party at Wetherspoons. Richard and I did meet up a few months later, he was getting married and I had an invitation from that first meeting. Our relationship got stronger and all the fourteen years faded away, we have not looked back.

As I approached the next two jobs in my life, unexceptional things happened which I have to share with you. Spirit holds no bounds. We have now acquired another puppy, she is a white boxer with brindle around the eyes, she actually came to us by surprise. A lady who we knew from the cafe was looking for a home for her and as it was now a year since we lost Tammy, our German shepherd dog, it just seemed the right time. Jane, the lady told me it was a bulldog, lovely, I thought, then when we went to see her I said Jane that's not a bulldog, it's a boxer. We all laughed. It was John's birthday and Daisy, the boxer, was four months old, she seemed right for us and at that time, I was at a loose end as to what I wanted to do as a job so it was a great opportunity to get to know

Daisy, she was a handful at first but she was always game for whatever you wanted to do, life would not be the same again.

I did still do some readings on and off, which helped fill the gaps of day-to-day living. All of a sudden, I had this yearning to go back to cooking so I started looking at the adverts in the local paper, one week an advert jumped out at me. Cooking has played a very large part in my life as when I left school I went to catering college and so here I was again looking for that special job again. As we left the cafe, it would be great to get stuck into it again. Anyway, this advert that jumped out at me was a hotel a sort of sailors rest if you like, it was based at Tilbury Essex about seven miles away, it basically gave sailors a home for the rest of their lives if they had nowhere else to go, after they left the sea when they retired. The job was well paid but very different, a challenge, I was given the job and I took it on because I was drawn to this massive building somehow, why? I do not know, it may be because my dad was in the navy, a deep-sea diver and he drew me there but it looked exciting.

It was not until I had been there a couple of months, strange feelings would occur it seemed like each time I went to work these strange things would happen to me and then it became apparent the sailors hotel was going to close down, as they could not keep it going, too expensive as it was such a large building to maintain, just as I was getting to know the job and the people. Anyway, one morning one of the housekeepers found Mick (one of the old seafarers) had passed over and died in the night, the poor girl was in shock. It was not until after his funeral that I kept feeling somebody spiritual was in the kitchen with me, after asking who was there, as I kept feeling that I was being watched then I realised it was Mick he told me he did not want to leave, I said he had to go into the spirit world as that is where he belonged now, he said he was very worried about the hotel and the seafarers that were his friends. Not long after this, a very strange occurrence happened to two of the housekeepers even I could not explain it, the girls could not understand it either, both of them going into the lift to come down after their days work, they did the same each day, as they got into the lift it was twelve o'clock when they got out it was 1 o'clock and both of them could not explain where that hour had gone, they both came running into the kitchen white as a sheet they were hoping I could explain what happened but as I said I could not, the only thing I could think of was perhaps it was a moment in time where it stopped just for them, a psychic event where something happened hundreds of years ago. If anyone out there has an explanation, I am willing to listen. Going back to Mick, he said that they are all being turfed out of their home, he seemed very impatient and demanding. I told him they would find other places to live but I felt at this moment whatever I said, he would hang around. I knew that my job was not safe and that I would eventually move on so I started once again to search for another job but before I move on from the hotel, I was to have another spiritual encounter but this time it involved Tina, who worked at the hotel as well. I became friendly with Tina because she was very interested in spiritual communication and eventually met her husband Peter, he then became involved, his father had passed into spirit a year before and Peter came to see me after he had experienced a strange dream. Tina at first asked me if I could help. Ronald Quayle Hughes, Peter's dad, wanted to talk to him so he came to Peter in a dream. I thought the best way would be for Tina to bring along a personal item so I could do a reading for him by using this item to tune in as reading, I decided the best place would be in the hotel but chose somewhere secure as the place was already full of activity. I wanted to make sure the communication coming in was as right as it could be. They both came one evening after work and brought a pair of glasses that were his dad's, as I took them I heard Peter's father chuckle and a laugh, I asked him what he was laughing at, he said those glasses were not the only pair he had there was another pair that broke just before he died. At the time, Peter and Tina did not know what he was talking about until they returned home and this was indeed confirmed. Peter's father also came through with a John, he mentioned John was there to meet him when he passed over, apparently, John was his best friend, he had passed six years before but Ronald and John were cremated on the same day six years apart. Peter and Tina told me that just before his father died they had had a big discussion about their friend John and he had said he would have liked to have got to know John a little better, funnily enough on the day Peter's father passed away he had said to them, I hope John is there to meet me and it looked like he got his wish. As further validation Peter's Father wanted to mention Bill to us, a man who is also special to us, Bill is my father, Tina said and of course, Peter's father-in-law. Ronald, Peter's father said he was so pleased Gemma, Tina and Peter's daughter had continued to visit her grandmother after he had died. This would to some people feel a bit strange for him to say but Gemma was extremely close to her grandfather and would spend the whole time of her visit with him and not so much with her grandmother. She loves her dearly but after Ronald had died she had said she did not want to visit anymore, Tina and Peter eventually persuaded her that her grandfather would want her to visit her grandmother and would be really sad if she did not. Tina also said that Rita (me) said Peter loved his garden, loved growing runner beans but was not very good at D.I.Y and also had a love of boats, they both shared Tina validated that it was all true, also Peter's Mother loved bargain hunting and also talked about the changes made to the house. Peter's mother had never had a dream about her husband but Rita said she had had one recently when she was unwell where he visited her at night and sat on her bed. When Peter saw his mother recently, he asked her about the dream and she said yes why? So Peter told her about the reading. This just goes to show that readings not only help the sitters you are reading but sometimes the whole family.

My new start after leaving the hotel for the old sailors was at a children's nursery and brought to me new people, new eager faces willing and wanting to know about life after death, although this was a little different. Lisa who worked at the nursery, I knew, in fact, she pushed for me to get the job, it was cooking again but for nursery children, one extreme to the other I suppose, but this was to be a new experience for me because as soon as I stepped into the building, I felt as if someone or something spiritual did not want me there, it felt like I was a threat to them, which I was to a certain extent unknown to me. I talked to Lisa about it, she was the girl I mentioned earlier in my book where her friend J.J had been killed in the water by drowning. Lisa liked me being at the nursery, I think I made her feel closer to J.J, at this moment in time. Anyway, as we chatted about the strange feelings, I was getting at the nursery, I suddenly saw a very stern man standing all alone, he told me he had lived in a caravan years ago on the site where the nursery stood now. He said he was a gipsy, he came every year because there would be gipsy council meetings in Aveley, where all the gipsies would come from all over the country. One night, he told me he had had an argument with another man on the nursery site and he got stabbed and killed, then they put him inside his caravan and set light to it, at this Lisa said she could smell burning in the babies' room in the back and could not understand why? This was the room that when I approached, it made me feel sick and dizzy, luckily at that time, when I worked, it was in the kitchen area, no tiny babies here, so no spirits in here but they do follow me around. A strange thing happened one day in the babies' room, there was a microwave in there to heat the babies' milk, there was nothing wrong with the machine when all of a sudden it caught fire with no warning at all, we managed to get staff and children out, nobody was hurt. It was all okay. The only thing damaged was, of course, the microwave, which was replaced. I did try with all my resources to get this spirit to move but he would not budge, so I had to give up, as far as I know, today he is still there.

My son Dean, who was married to Sarah, I had mentioned about him earlier in my book, they were both desperate to have a baby, Sarah asked me if I had any thoughts or anything that will give her hope of having a baby in the future, will I ever conceive? She asked me, I tuned in to the spirit world to ask but nothing was given to me. I was really disappointed, I thought to myself, I never get anything for my own family but as I said to myself if I cannot get anything for her, that was it. I forgot about it for a while and then about three months later, one night I had a dream and in this dream, I was walking down a hospital corridor next to John, my husband as I looked at him I noticed he was holding a baby but in front were two more people holding another baby but I could not see who they were. In my mind I thought crumbs, it looks like they are going to have twins but to me, it did not seem as if it was going to happen yet. I told Sarah about the dream and she told me there had been twins in the family on her side, so it could happen, the dream did not come true for another six years.

In those six years, many changes were to take place for Dean and Sarah and for John and myself, as for this year and into the next which was 2003, which was a fabulous year, seeing Richard my son again was a happy time for me, he mentioned that he was getting married next year August 2004 and that, of course, he wanted me and John to be there. During that time, my clairvoyance became more intense and I was able to help a lot of people. One of them was Donna, who lived in Stanford-le-Hope, Essex this was about six miles away from where I live now, it also played a big part in my earlier life with my ex-husband Norman, my two boys went to school there, played football and also grew up in that part of the world but as I mentioned in my first book, it was an unhappy time for me, as Norman was having an affair with a young girl of seventeen, which lasted six years. Today people would not put up with adultery but back in the seventies, it actually was not that easy to just pick up sticks and go so it was that you put up with it and keep quiet, in fact, I had nobody to turn to in my hour of need and eventually it nearly pushed me over the edge and if I had not met John when I did, I do not know where I would be today. I know spirit had a hand in this. Maybe my mum or dad helped me to meet John and change my life, eventually.

Anyway, going back to Donna, I felt she needed me in a big way, I had to go to her house as she was having problems with a housebound spirit. Apparently, she had got my number through the local paper when I had my story told, so here I was back in Stanford-le-Hope, I found her house tucked away in a cul-de-sac, as soon as I saw Donna, I knew we were going to be friends and even to this day years later, we still keep in touch. On approaching her living room, it felt cold, although it looked wonderful with a beautiful colour of lilac and candles everywhere to the naked eye, it looked very relaxing and spiritual, but to me suddenly the atmosphere was heavy. I asked Donna if I could go around the house and make myself known to the spirits that were there watching us, I did not think the one that was being mischievous was in the living room. As we went upstairs, the back bedroom showed great promise of spiritual activity. This room, Donna told me, she could not go in, it felt unhappy and it seemed the spirit did not and would not go. The spirit talked about a lady that lived there and was very unhappy in the room we mentioned, a feeling of being unloved, unwanted. I tuned in told her that she could now move on because she is loved by the people surrounding her from the world beyond, I think she said everything she wanted to say as no more details came through. I said a prayer and showed her the light and as she looked, Donna and myself joined hands and felt her go to her family in the afterlife, I then stayed with Donna for a while chatting, had a coffee, enjoyed our time together and then said our farewells. Later in the week, I had a lovely card from Donna thanking me for my help, she also told me how relieved she was now that the problem had been sorted, she also said it was a great experience for her and now the room feels normal and she can go into the back bedroom now without that awful feeling. I was so pleased that is what my work is all about half of the time, to see people happy and content makes it all worthwhile.

John and I and Daisy, our boxer dog now three years old, decided to rent a holiday cottage in Snape Suffolk. It was on the grounds of a large old farmhouse, which suited us down to the ground. Unknown to me, this holiday was going to change the course of our lives. Over the past few months, I was getting recurring dreams of walking the streets looking at houses but then I would wake up and think why would I be moving to an old house, when I loved the house we were in the newness of the style, everything about it and I used to think how lucky I was to be living here. Getting back to the holiday, it was relaxing, Daisy had a bit of a garden to run around in and the walks were endless. Three days into the holiday, we decided to make our way to Aldeburgh, it was about seven miles away from where we were staying. As we made our way out onto the A12, I then saw a sign for Lowestoft, I then said to John, 'Oh look, we are only Twenty-Five miles away. Perhaps we could go tomorrow for a change', John agreed. After a nice day in Aldeburgh, we got ourselves ready for the next day. Of course, we had to take Daisy with us as we were unable to leave her alone in the cottage.

Today the weather was on our side and on arriving in Lowestoft we had to stay near the beach, Daisy, as usual, going mad on the sands, playing in the water and doing crazy things that boxers do, she had already had one of her crucial ligaments in one of her back legs replaced but that did not deter her. She enjoys every minute of her life as we walked along with the front John and I could smell the aroma of fish and chips, it did not take much for us to find the shop where the lovely smell was coming from, John stayed with Daisy while I went in the shop to buy our lunch as I waited for them to be cooked, I started talking to a lady behind the counter about the properties in Lowestoft and could not believe how cheap they were in this area when I came out carrying the fish and chips I told John about it, he said crumbs we could sell our house and buy one here and not have a mortgage, I laughed not realising then how true all this would become.

Within the next few months, the firm John was working for pulled the plug on the drivers. This made us realise he would soon be out of work. We had enough money to keep us going till about October 2004. It was early April, now that dream I kept having was going to become a reality. John put it to me, perhaps now was the time to move, which of course, Lowestoft was in his mind, also Richard and Suzanne were getting married this year but I knew nothing was going to stop me from getting to their wedding the date was August 28' which was their day so it was all happening very, very fast. John's mum and dad offered to stay with Daisy, the dog so we could make our way to Lowestoft in search of our new or old home to be, as my dream foretold, we walked the streets looking and looking desperate, trying to find something amongst these strange and unusual houses. Our house was sold and we needed to move fast as the people who had bought ours were first-time buyers and we really did not want them to pull out on us, as John was without a job, our money was being gobbled up. We eventually found a house in St. Peter's Street but unknown to us, we did not realise how bad the house was till we moved in, it really was awful. The moving date was a week after Richard's wedding, the day of the wedding was lovely, of course, I was a little worried about the reaction of my ex-husband Norman's family but as far as I knew then, all was okay. It was great being part of Richard's life again.

September 3 dawned, our big move day, everybody came to say goodbye, we were now leaving our house in Essex and going into the unknown of another part of the country, new people, not knowing what lies ahead, would I still be able to do my spiritual work? Would we find jobs? Would we be happy? Surely Spirit would want this for me, I have to put my trust in them. At some point over the past couple of months, I was hoping John would change his mind or perhaps the people buying our house would pull out, if I could sum up how I felt, I felt scared. I loved the house we were leaving, family, and friends, everything I had known for the past twenty-seven years. Today there is no going back, Lowestoft, here we come!

Chapter Three

When we reached Lowestoft and the house on St. Peter's Street, I could not believe what I saw. As I opened the front door, the smell hit me. The carpet that was left in the middle dining room had to be lifted up and thrown outside because it was full of dog mess, we then had to scrub the floor before we could get any of our furniture off the van to put into the house. I could have cried, what have we done? The house was ours but I took an instant dislike to it. John tried to console me, saying as soon as we decorate and make it our own things would improve. I realise I was being taught a valuable lesson here. We cannot always have what we want in life. Also, those material things are only what we have here in life, we do not need them when we go into the world of spirit.

John did what he promised and I helped, of course. We cleaned, we decorated, we moved a shower and toilet upstairs to make it easier on ourselves, while John was busy doing that, I decided to walk up the high street, for something to do really but as I looked into people's faces milling about, in my mind, I did not at that time feel part of it. I expect a lot of people reading this have been in the same situation, so they know how it feels, although in the world we have today with mobile phones and the internet it would be different but not so much back then.

One day, I decided to walk to what is called the Sparrow's nest so-called because sailors were stationed there in the last war, in the east of Britain and it got well bombed, people had at that time gone through so much, I strictly told myself when I read the memorial on the people who had died for our country that these humble beings survived at some lengths, for peace and also some of the sailors died far away from their loved ones.

Lowestoft is the most easterly town in Britain, there is so much history here dating back to times past before the navy before the world wars. The older generations around here have their stories to tell of times gone by, their hopes and dreams they had then of a better future, from the fishermen who put their lives at risk for a crust of bread. Now that the future is here with a massive new ASDA store, the jobs are different for the youngsters of today but the community spirit is still here if you look for it. Going down the streets called the scores give you a sense of the past, they are just off the old high street. Thinking about the past booted me into my future, kicking myself, I told myself off in a way, we do not live on the moon, I heard myself saying (I think my friends in spirit had something to do with that).

I, at last, found a job in the housekeeping department at a Gunton Hall a Warners Holiday Camp which was good, it all started to feel more friendly, as I walked the dog, Daisy, people would stop to say hello and they stopped to chat, it felt good but the house I could not love, it felt alien to me the walls seemed to close in on me, it made me feel lonely I missed my friends back in Essex. I knew I had to deal with it in my own way, how would I be able to do my spiritual work again if I felt like this, where would I meet people that needed me again?

After three months, John was able to get a job in a hotel called The Wherry as a kitchen porter, it was in Oulton Broad, about two miles away from where we live, it led to him getting his NVQ one and two in cooking then he went on to do the third one. I stayed at Gunton Hall for a few months, where I did make a couple of friends. Funny enough it was where we stayed once on holiday in the past and there I was working in the same place, but after a while I was getting these feelings of wanting to work with the older generation but before moving on, I have to tell you about another strange thing that happened to me (I hear you saying there's no change there then).

It was the Christmas of 2004, there was a staff party, on the night we were given a free raffle ticket as they had a raffle for all the staff and to my amazement, I won one of the tickets and it was a radio plus C.D. This was a blast from the past because a couple of years ago, I did a cleaning job for a gentleman by the name of Pat and on the last Christmas I worked for him, I bought him a new radio as the one he had, the sound was really bad he was chuffed with it as he did not possess a Television and the radio was all he had. Two months later he passed away, John said, are you going to take the radio back but I said no let the family have it, it did not seem right somehow. On getting this radio as a prize, it was like Pat was giving the radio back to me as it was the exact same one as I had bought him, I still have that radio today.

In February, I made a work change, I saw in the local paper about a company named one to one. It did a service where you go out to the elderly and help them in their own homes with things they cannot do for themselves by doing this work you give them the help they need but they still stay in their familiar surroundings and also can still have their own independence. I joined the company and I did learn a lot with them, it was giving me the knowledge for when I was going on to do my last job before I retired. Unknown to me at the time, I felt I just needed time so I could start thinking about doing my spiritual work and this job did not give me that but working in the community gave me a lot of experience and as I looked around, there was a job going in a care home. This job was cooking once again but I had the best of two worlds, one that I could go back to what I loved and two the residents were in need of care and I helped with that at times and best of all, I had time off which gave me the opportunity to decide about what I could do on the spiritual side. At the care home, which was called east view, I found a friend with the same name as myself Rita (yes another one) she made me feel very much at home in Lowestoft also we put the house we were in on the market and decided we would move to Oulton Broad which was two miles out of Lowestoft.

At the end of 2005, we actually sold the house I hated and bought a small bungalow, it was the place I had seen in a dream before we moved up here. In the dream, John and I were walking the streets looking at property when we came upon a side gate as we looked around the back I could see the whole back was patio doors and the garden was full of ornaments as we went around the front, we sat on a grass lawn which seemed to go downhill. Well, it had all of that in the dream, the feel of the grass that went down was because we were on top of a road that went down, how cool is that sometimes we have to put the puzzle together to see the whole picture. Rose, who lived here until she died, I felt loved in this place as well although, it had a good feeling she has never shown herself to me, I believe that she is happy now with her husband in spirit, he had passed some years before Rose and now they are together. Here we have the river which is the broads, the boats, and we are also not too far from the shops in Lowestoft and the seafront, as we found out also there were lovely walks for Daisy, the dog and when we moved in, Daisy went really mad running around in the lovely big garden, it was lovely to watch her, oh, I said if Daisy was happy so were we.

After a few months of moving in, the spiritual communications started again, I was happy in my job, happy in my home, it just goes to show when life is better and your mind is clear, communication can come in. Going back in my mind, I remember what my friend Joan told me years ago (she is now in spirit) that one day I would run a circle and there would be one man in it. This did actually happen but it all came about as I decided to advertise in the local paper, I met loads of interesting people through readings and they all went well and it was through this I met Chloe.

Chloe Story of Events.

I arranged to see Chloe one Tuesday evening at six. The reading was to take a strange turn, she did actually arrive a bit later than planned but there was a reason for that, they were working their magic in the spirit world. The reading started to go well, giving her some good advice on things going on in her life, then a young gentleman at exactly 6.45 pm stood in the way (from the spirit world, of course). I tried to ignore him but he would not let me. He kept on at me nudging me a couple of times to get my attention and then said, "I died in a motorbike accident", as I told Chloe this she was over the moon at this statement, her brother (I will call him Sean) died a year earlier on that exact same day at 6.45 pm, the time he came through nudging me. The whole story came out, he was travelling towards Norwich not speeding at all, as he came to a junction in the road a tractor pulled out in front of him and instead of Sean stopping he decided to go around it but it had a trailer on the back and that is what caused his death. After that night Chloe and I became friends and between us, we decided to start a circle at my home.

It was through Chloe another lady by the name of Lyn came along, interested in working with spirit, Lyn already had loads of knowledge about spiritual matters because her whole life since she was eight years old, she had known they were there she could see them and hear them and they had taken over her whole life. It was heaped upon her, the day she came along with Chloe. I had never actually known it before but as the weeks passed and the circle became strong, so did the spirit on her shoulders lifted, making her feel better and live a much happier life. Also, she began to understand how to deal with the wonderful gift she has, Lyn was actually finding her feet again. Then Jill came along to circle and finally the man by the name of Mick. This was obviously the man Joan had seen all those years ago. I can see her looking down on me and nodding, (I told you so).

It was a good circle as we all helped each other. I would start with a prayer leading to opening all 7 psychic centres, this makes way for the spirit to enter. We also do healing, which is very important, healing can be done in the room or absent healing, this is where you put names in a book and then read them out and ask for that healing to be sent to the person involved. Also in a circle, we ask about learning the pathways we have to take in life, we then do spiritual walks and meditation, on the closing of the circle we say a closing prayer then make sure we close ourselves down so there are no comebacks from our spirit friends, I always say if I did not have this special gift and ability it would not be me also I would miss it in my life, you do find your way forward from new beginnings. I never go out looking for the spirit, it always finds me, which brings me to tell you about psychic suppers.

I thought it would be a good idea to do these suppers like we used to in the churches years ago but in people's houses, they can invite their friends to an evening of clairvoyance, where I would challenge myself and my guides. It was actually through a lady by the name of Kay, she was another person who joined my circle; she was good at drawing and photography. I always felt although she was with us it was only a matter of time before she moved on but at that time, it was Kay who started the psychic suppers off for me in her house, the hostess supplies the food and drink and invites her friends. I then come in and usually bring envelopes, I then ask all who come to put something in the envelope like a picture a piece of jewellery that can be your own or belonged to a loved one in spirit, I keep the envelope till the end as sometimes this helps to give the person it belongs to something special. I first go round the room giving each person there about ten to fifteen minutes of clairvoyance then after they have had their supper, it makes it a good evening to then open the envelope myself not knowing whose it is I have opened, it works so well and everybody enjoys the evening. On one occasion, there were three ladies sitting on the sofa together, I could see that one of them was pregnant I got the feeling of twins, which I mentioned to her, she said no only one, 'my friend is having a baby perhaps you picked up on her as well', okay I said but I did not feel it was right (I bumped into her two years later and she told me you never guess I had twins, spirit move in a remarkable way). It also proves that we live beyond this world.

The energy that comes through sometimes is unbelievable, on many occasions I surprised myself but trust is always there on one of the evening suppers, I had a funny experience as a gentleman who came along was carrying a large Teddy Bear and I did not know until I gave out the envelopes why he had that bear until he said I cannot fit this bear in an envelope, it brought about loads of laughter all around the room lifting everyone's spirit and it relaxed everybody making it a lovely evening, by the way, the man did get a bit of reading from the teddy as I held it, which satisfied him so it just goes to show help is always on hand. All these meetings bring in friends and these friends make it happen. Lives that get turned upside down are put right again from a simple message from a loved one.

It is now the year 2006 Dean (my youngest son) decided to move to Lowestoft, much to my delight they found a lovely big bungalow over the bridge from where we are on the south of Lowestoft and John and I helped them to move in. It was a long day, but as they say, moving can be very stressful anyway. It was great to have them close. After a couple of months, Dean found a job driving for a meat firm and they settled down. I then had the dream again about a baby being born. If you remember, I spoke about it earlier in the book, well this dream now was reality and it was not what I expected, it all became clear in a very strange way. In the next year 2007, Richard and Susanne, they actually still live in Essex, (Richard being my eldest) came up to see us here with the wonderful news that Susanne was pregnant. Hooray! After all this time, I was going to be a nan. I felt happy but also felt sad for Dean and Sarah who at that time, had been trying for fourteen years to no avail, then out of the blue six weeks later, Dean phones me with the good news, Sarah after all those years had become pregnant as well, six weeks between them going back to my dream earlier in my book seeing the two babies thinking it might be twins, just six weeks different so it was obvious the two people walking in front was Richard and Susanne and us at the back for Dean and Sarah, well? Just believe what you see and it does happen even if at that time you do not understand it. The two baby girls were born in February 2008 and April 2008, how great was that dream. The trust you have to have in spirit shows no bounds. This has made me trust in the dreams I have, more. We all have that communication and we have to open our eyes to see it.

Today the dreams come hard and fast, especially when I do my psychic suppers as I always get given something in a dream that will tell me where to start on those special evenings. The circle is going well, even Daisy joins in from time to time, she just sits there in between as if she is part of the circle, it was while I was out walking Daisy that I met Cindy. I kept bumping into her and one day I said would you like to walk with us? She agreed and we eventually became good friends.

Just before I leave this chapter of psychic suppers, I have to tell you what happened at the Carlton Manor. John, my husband worked there as a chef for a while, it was a place where people stayed for the night and also it was a restaurant, arrangements were made for me to do a psychic supper at this venue, I asked for help from another medium because I thought it might be too much to do on my own, what an evening it turned out to be. We had only catered for about sixty people but the word must have got around us on the night, at least one hundred and fifty people turned up food ran out and the kitchen struggled, I was so glad I had asked Olive, the other medium to help, the evening went really well in the end and we had some good evidence, the world of spirit worked well for us that night the atmosphere was electric and I can honestly say we had fun, we worked hard and played hard and it was good. There was a spirit in one of the bedrooms there, I was asked to go into this room as I did so, on the window was a word help! 'Oh, I said look at that!' Everybody ran from the room and left me with this spirit who I believed wanted help to go into the spirit world so I prayed and asked for her family to come in and take her on her journey to the afterlife, I never heard any more so hopefully she is at peace now.

Chapter Four

Rose's Story

I suddenly got a phone call out of the blue from a lady by the name of Rose. The call was frantic "help help", I am in the bathroom and I dare not come out, there is a ghost in my house, I have three children in here with me, one is only a baby, we are all in here because we are scared to come out please, please come as soon as you can. As I looked at the clock, it was 7.30 pm. She lived in Beccles, which is about eight miles away from my house, at that time I did not know the area. I jumped in the car to my amazement and with a little help from above, I found the address Rose gave me, I was a bit apprehensive, a little unsure what I would find when I got there, as I knocked on the door Rose had managed to come out of the bathroom, they were all a bit shaken up, I managed to calm them all down apparently one of her daughters had seen a man a few times in her bedroom. On tuning in to this man, he was bold as brass because he said this is my house, he had a right to be there I want them gone, I told him in no certain terms that he had passed into the spirit world and it was somebody else's house now but just as in life he was a stubborn person, he would not really harm anyone but I felt he had lost his way and although I managed to clear things that night, I had a feeling he would be back.

Two weeks later, as I expected, another call came from Rose, this time she said it was worse as there were two of them now, poor Rose not only was she a new mother trying to now cope with three children but she had this to contend with as well, (sometimes I find with a new addition to the family, it opens up a void to let spirit in if you are open to it as each new baby is born and as they come from the spirit world, a door opens up a bit like a vortex and sometimes it let in the mischief spirit in as in Rose's case). As I tuned in, this time, another man came in and said he lives next door. Apparently, the whole story came out that the two men used to argue a lot over the garden fence and looking at them both they had not changed. I mentioned quietly that they were both in spirit now and they must settle their differences so they can move on in the spirit world as they have their families waiting for them, it took a lot of energy and a lot of praying but in the end, it paid off, they did see the light above and moved forward, the atmosphere changed in the room, it also seemed happier and it calmed down, actually the second man who lived next door had only been here for past three weeks, this is why on my first visit I only picked up with the one man. Rose was really pleased anyway and while I was there she asked for a reading for herself, it was through this reading that we made contact with her nan when I met her again a couple of weeks later.

Her nan told me, Rose had been through some terrible times lately with an ex-partner who was the children's dad which is personal to her which her nan described but she was also told to look forward and her nan also said she was to look forward as she was about to meet a man at the school gates and they would be together and happy, she would also move and there would be more children coming into her life. At the time, I do not think she believed what I was saying to her. I felt she was in a dark place, no way was she at that time thinking that things would change. Over the next few months, I did not see Rose then out of the blue she phoned me again asking for a reading and I am afraid it came up the same sort of reading, obviously, things had not changed yet, I think she just wanted some upliftment if you like and boy did they give it, her nan had centre stage again giving her love and confirmation that things were going to change, Rose had been through hell and she needed time to adjust before she would finally see the light at the end of the tunnel.

All three years have passed since that first meeting with Rose, yes that is how far ahead of some of the readings can be before they finally emerge into our life. After all this, I visited her again but this time it was different, there standing before me, was a happy and excited Rose. "I have met someone," she said, as I entered the hallway (as if I could not guess the happiness radiating from her). As I sat down and we started to talk this tall man stood in the doorway, his name was Ian, as I looked at them both I felt Rose was going to have a baby and it would be a boy, she then laughed as you remember she had three girls, then I laughed with her because Ian came back carrying a baby boy in his arms, Ian's wife had gone into a coma while pregnant, Ian had asked for the baby to go full term before the life support was turned off. He was then, of course, left to bring up the baby on his own, how awful that he has had to go through all that but I am sure his wife in spirit, brought Rose and Ian together and now they have each other, always working up there in the next world, some people might say its fate.

A week later, I got a text from Rose to say she was pregnant, and yes guess what, she had a baby boy, now they have five children, Ian is a marvellous dad to all of them but the house was too small for all of them. Ian had a house that belonged to him and his wife and eventually, he sold the house and bought a wonderful five-bedroom house, so never, ever, disbelieve what spirit tells you in your readings because things do change for the better. In your darkest moments look towards the light, although Rose did learn a lot and so did I, now she is helping a lot of people in the same situation as she was in and in her ways, she tells people about me and then they want a reading as well, I call it snowballing. The last I heard of Rose, she and Ian got married. Lovely happy ending. Through Rose, I met Emma, this brings me to another wonderful story.

Emma's Story

Emma arranged to have a reading with me one morning (she also lived in Beccles). I knocked on the door, I got barked at as she had two dogs and of course, their bark was worse than their bite but they were there to protect her and I soon found a way into the dog's hearts, I just love dogs whatever the breed. I was surprised as I walked into the lounge as she had a friend there with her, this first reading went well, she had some good evidence come through and at the end of her reading, her friend got some as well, then all of a sudden a spirit appeared at the bottom of the stairs that I could see from where I was sitting, the spirit was covered in this orange glow, Emma said the children had seen this lady as well and they were very scared. As soon as I heard that, I knew deep down I had to see this through.

As I tuned into the orange looking lady, the whole story came out, back in the 1900s, there was a factory where the houses that Emma lived in were built, on the land where the factory stood back then. In 1912, the lady told me the factory burnt down, the fire escape was locked and this poor lady could not get out and she was burnt to death at the top of the stairs. That is what the orange was all about (it was her engulfed in flames). I then thanked her for talking to us, I got Emma and her friend to join in a circle around this lady and showed her the way into the spirit world. It worked and then I felt a sense of peace. Emma went to the library to see what she could find about the land her house was built on and lo-and-behold, all that was said was right, I knew then that at some point I would be going back.

When Emma next got in touch, I hoped she would be on her own, as the last time her reading was not finished and it felt as if it should be private to her. As soon as I sat down again, hoping to give her a better reading she was on her own and a spirit appeared straight away, apparently ten years ago, she had a little boy with Steve, he was her soulmate who she loved more than life itself but they were into drugs at that time and her little boy was taken off of her. One fateful day Steve went missing, Emma searched for him and to her horror, she found him dead on his boat on the river, close to where they lived. As I saw all this happening, I could see fields, horses, loads of trees, and a very peaceful place. Steve was showing me all of this, as it was the last thing he saw before he passed over. It broke her heart and on this second meeting, Emma kept saying she wanted her boy back that they had shared together. I could see this twelve-year-old boy (Steve was showing me). Emma said she had always kept in touch with him as she now had other children but of course the guilt she has is always with her. Today, though, she is completely off drugs and trying to sort herself out with, of course, Steve's help from the spirit world. I was told by her loved one's in spirit that her boy would come back to live with her, which cheered her up no end but before I got to that over the next year there was something else that needed to be done.

Over the next year or so, there was a lot of work to be done regarding the fire in the factory from years before, that I talked about earlier, I had to go back to Emma's time and time again as the fire had started where Emma's house had stood and there were many people that had passed away that fateful day wanting to get my attention. As I sat, her living room was filled with the faces of spirit people everywhere. They all had a longing in their eyes, I could see a look of why did it happen to me! I then gathered them all together and I had to explain we are now in the year 2012, one hundred years later and they all need to now go into the world of spirit to fulfil their dreams and then one by one as I prayed they left the scene of devastation along with the awful memories of their passing. Now, as I look on, I can see they are all happy again, catching up with their loved ones in the next world. Emma commented on how much better her house feels now.

There was just another thing I have to tell you before I move on, I did go back to Emma's as she asked for another reading a little later, after all the hustle and bustle with the spirits, it seemed important somehow because as I started the reading Steve once again came in very loud and clear with a warning, "Be careful when a stranger comes to the door, do not open," he was very adamant on this he said, "I will protect you." I heard later in the year that apparently one morning about 6.30 am Emma was sitting downstairs having a cuppa and a cigarette like she normally does before the children get up when there was a knock on the door, her first instincts flowed in, first, you want to go to see who it is, then she suddenly stopped remembered the warning in her reading, 'Do not open the door'. As she went into the kitchen, there was a man's face at the window peering in, she actually knew the man's face but would not open the door, in the end, he went away. Sometime later, Emma heard that a woman further down the road had answered her door and got attacked and raped by the same man she had seen, Emma was able to give the police a good description of the man that she had seen and eventually he was caught and sent to prison. That day was the day that Steve protected her from the spirit world, oh yes, her son, her firstborn, had also been coming home to stay on and off getting closer to his mum, happiness for all. It's so rewarding doing this psychic work when you are there through the bad and then a light is switched on, not looking back from now on only forward, Steve was Emma's soul mate and always will be until they meet once again in the afterlife, he did say at one point that she would meet someone in the future but when it was her turn to pass over, they would be together. Cannot ask for more from the spirit world, can I?

Sorry this is not the end to Emma's story as just recently, I went to see her again and as I went again into her sitting room, it was like walking into a dense fog of spirit, a feeling of something awful had happened this was after I gave her a reading once again, which I feel went really well again, the atmosphere gained strength around us I mentioned to Emma it feels like a murder has happened after the fire in 1912, of course, she did say the land that the factory was on was left derelict for many years so anything could have happened as there were a lot of homeless people living on the site so it could have happened then. I felt this man wanted justice for his death as he did not get it at the time of his passing, I felt at that time it could have been in the 60s or 70s, for this we will have to wait and see what emerges in the future, (watch this space). I suddenly felt there was a vortex emerging in the middle of the room this is a doorway between the two worlds, it can happen anywhere all over the world, the spirit can come and go as they please, then through this doorway, a man in uniform appeared he mentioned a base where he was stationed and he had come from a base near Emma's house. Emma said that is strange as yesterday she had walked over the back of her house with the dogs and over there is a spot where a plane had come down and crashed in the war, I put this down to her picking up the airman while she was there and he then wanted to communicate knowing I was coming here today, I tell you there is so much going on in the area where she lives perhaps I could pick up more but it will have to wait, it looks like in the future another soul will be laid to rest through our circle rescue.

Mandy's Story

Mandy got in touch with me the same way as the others through word of mouth. It is a wonder my ears are not burning all the time through the talk of others. Mandy, at that time, was feeling very low, her ex-partner was hounding her day and night, in fact, all the time, the police were involved and she was really down. In her reading, I tried to lift her spirit telling her she would meet someone soon it would be on the internet (where else in this day with all the electronic equipment we have) her nan was there giving her advice, she also told Mandy that things will be sorted out soon and she could start living again. I do not think she believed me totally at that time but other things I said to her from her nan, especially to do with her autistic son, this made her start thinking about what I had said. As things that I had mentioned in her reading started to surface, Mandy got in touch again wanting another reading and her mum, June wanted to come as well as it was her mum that came through last time and June was interested as to know what she was going to say next, in fact, she had lots to say and over the next couple of years June's mum took the limelight, during one of the last readings with June something wonderful came in, she told me about a pub that June owned with her husband in the old town in Lowestoft next to the pub, was a cottage that they lived in while running the business. One day, they decided to take down a wall in the cottage to make the room bigger and as they did so inside the wall, they found an anchor from a large ship. They told people about this find and were told not to remove it as it would bring them bad luck but word got out and the powers that got to hear about it so they had to surrender the anchor to the authorities, June or I will never know what became of it. The trouble was after that June and her husband got divorced, was it bad luck associated with the anchor? Or would it have happened, anyway? Which is what

I believe anyway, that your life is mapped out and we make our own luck in life, be it good or bad.

After that exciting reading June wanted another sitting back with me in the house, she had moved to in the middle of Beccles apparently her son-in-law and his family also lived with her but it was the son-in-law that kept seeing a man in the bathroom in this house, especially when he was looking in the mirror, as I looked at the address I could not believe my eyes, it was the same place I went to eight years ago to do an afternoon of clairvoyance similar to the psychic suppers I do in the evening but it was a different family as June had only been there a couple of years. The bathroom was on the ground floor at the back of the property and she just wanted to know who it was that was frightening her son-in-law. I went into the area of the bathroom and stood in the middle. As I did, so the whole story came out. Years ago it felt like the eighties or nineties, the house was used for students, the spirit man told me he was gay and at that era, it was not so well known and he got some stick about it all the time, one evening he got into a fight out in the garden where the bathroom now stood, a knife was involved and this man who was haunting the bathroom got killed in that spot, apparently it was an outbuilding then and there was a cover-up of his death. I told him I was sorry but life has now moved on, he did not want to move on into the spirit world. So I expect he is still wondering about to this day, let's hope he sees the light soon and passes into the next world. I then gave June the usual reading, although I found it hard going but as usual, the spirit never let me down.

Going back to the end of Mandy's story because as you know we all like a happy ending, she had been through a lot with her ex-partner and the police were involved in so much of her life then but with the help of her loved ones in spirit, her life turned around when she met the love of her life on the internet but he was living in Exeter as on one of Mandy's last readings she told me she was moving to Exeter to be with her man and leaving the children here to be with their dad, her new partner lived and worked in that part of the country. She also at that time looked happy and relaxed, a different person so something must be right, I could not understand at this point why spirit did not mention about her moving, in fact, I got quite upset that it was not mentioned in the reading because it was a very important issue in her life all the way back home from Beccles, I kept asking why did spirit not give me this information? I kept doubting myself, I am not good enough? Why had spirit let me down and not given me the moving of Mandy when it was so important but lo-and-behold eleven days later after the move she had to come home back to her house again because one of her children who as I say they were with their dad became very ill with appendicitis and from that it was the same as before she came back home she had to be with her children and it was as if she had never been away, so an important lesson I learned that day for myself never doubted the spirit world because they know about the future more than we do. Mandy is still with her man and I did meet up with her once again a few years after and found out she had married the love of her life and was very happy, in fact, she was getting sorted to go and live with him in Exeter, taking the children who wanted to go with her. This was the last I saw of her.

Tracey's Story

The first memory I have of Tracey was of her waiting in my kitchen to come for a reading with me. The kitchen looks out in the garden so I could watch for her coming up the path. She worked with my husband John at a hotel called the Wherry. As I said before, it is situated not far from where we live now. Tracey was very interested in spiritual things, could be tarot cards, rune stones, future, everything even the healing side of things, which at this point did not appeal to me but Tracey changed all that giving me an insight into a different challenging world of spirit. Little did I know at that time, it would be the start of a lifelong friendship, although on our first meeting it did not feel like it, I thought her world was far away from mine, but over the years it changed. Sometimes you have to get to know the person before you can judge how you might feel. Anyway, on the first meeting, her reading went well to which I picked up with her friend Trudy who was dying of cancer at the end of the reading we talked a lot about spiritual things to which we helped each other a lot and then before she went Tracey asked me if I could give Trudy a reading this I arranged and during Trudy's reading I gave her a lot of insight into the world beyond, which made her feel at ease about dying and helped her understand in knowing where she was going. I did tell her she had a bit of time yet but there would come a time when she would give up on herself and join her loved ones in the next world.

On Tracey next visit after the passing of her friend Trudy, then as I looked into the world beyond Trudy told me there was going to be a wedding and it would be Tracey getting married I said to Tracey what her friend had said then it all came out yes she was about to get married, John and I got an invitation but I had a lot on and could not go. John went with other friends from the Wherry. Something deep inside of me said it's not going to work, she will not be happy, still, we have to learn by our own mistakes and I know as I have made quite a few along the way. I did not see Tracey anymore for a long time, although her daughter Lauren came to see me for a reading, it was during that time spirit told her that her mum would not be happy and she would get divorced. Tracey's marriage was not going to last.

The blow came three years later, when she found out her husband was seeing someone else, upon hearing this, I did what I could to help with all she was going through, at that time, I got a message from the spirit world to start doing the healing, I sort of knew what to do as we had been taught in the circle a lot of years ago when I was actually learning, after a lot of working at it, I gradually did learn how to do it and it worked, Tracey seemed very receptive to it. I gave her healing every week and I also noticed that while doing the healing, contact with spirit voices became stronger. The signs I get are my hands getting big like I have baseball gloves on. I can also feel a draught of air on the spot where there is pain on that person. It is wonderful really using the six senses that we all have, just as we were getting on track, Lauren, Tracey's daughter, had a breakdown. She went through a lot of stress and depression due to being raped at a young age by a family member. How much more can Tracey take, why Is this woman not grey yet? I helped with keeping her head straight and John helped by being there when needed as eventually Lauren had to go into hospital and he took them where they needed to go.

Tracey tells me now that she does not know how she kept it together but I know that her friend Trudy in spirit helped her from the other side, giving her strength when she needed it most. A lot of the time, it was hard knowing that she needed answers and I could not give them.

Now, as several years have passed, Lauren is well again and met a lovely man herself. She is happy and about to move in with this man. As for Tracey, she did eventually get divorced and we have now become good friends, I often go to her house to do my psychic suppers or she comes to me for spiritual guidance, men in her life as well, she does date now and she is more confident in herself. Let's hope she will meet someone special soon. I do have her to thank because she got me started on the healing as now I do it for others that come into my life and it seems to work (great). Although I am still working in the care home readings still come thick and fast, I fit them in as usual after my work or on days off. Sometimes, I feel tired but I do still need to keep my feet on the ground and my job helps with that.

My sister May moved up to Lowestoft in the year 2009 so we go out together at least once a week for coffee and shopping. My other sister Pauline moved to Wales, where all her family now live so because of that we do not see her quite so often. I do communicate with my dad who passed away in the spirit in 1980 but my mum I have heard very little from as she passed away in 1953 when I was six. Sometimes I do wonder what life would be like if things were different. I believe my nan, who was on my mother's side, had the same gift as me, but back then it was different and she was taken off to a mental asylum. Hard times then, but I am sure they are all there in spirit, edging me on while I am writing this book.

Chapter Five

I had seen the church in Pakefield just on the other side of Lowestoft as I took Daisy over there for our walks. Lovely beach, I felt this place where the church stood was a draw for me. Sometimes when I looked at it, I thought about the windows because they had plain glass in them, not the original ones made of coloured glass that you usually see in churches. My thoughts were to become a focus at work because I noticed that church would come into my mind a lot when I was on duty with a lady by the name of Linda. One day, while I was on my own with Linda, I told her about the church in Pakefield and how it seemed to be connected to herself as it kept coming into my space when I was working with her. Linda was surprised as she told me twenty years ago her sister was supposed to get married there but a fire put a stop to that and some of the windows were destroyed so it looked like that answered my thoughts about the windows, although I found out afterwards the poor church was also bombed in the war. I suppose it's because the church sits right on the seafront, making it a good target. Even after all that, it still feels like I get drawn to it.

I was sitting waiting for a lady to come on a reading with me by the name of Sue, in that time Pakefield and the church started to come into my mind again and as the reading, I mentioned to Sue that as I looked out of her bedroom window, I could see the sea, she told me yes that was right she lived in Pakefield near the sea, the reading went really well but all the time, I got this feeling that she was very scared of something going on around her at home, she did not tell me until after the reading apparently, her home was haunted and she did not know how to deal with it. As she left, I did say to her, if it still keeps on and you need my help, just give me a call. A couple of weeks later I did get that call from Sue and made an appointment to go over to her house to see what was going on there, at that time, in my mind the house I was going to was a cottage but as I pulled up outside, I was surprised to see a house that looked normal with the usual front to it as I went inside, I mentioned this to Sue and she said actually her house was a cottage but it had been built on at the front making it look much bigger. As I tuned in to the atmosphere, I felt like I needed to go right into the living room and as I did, there was this spirit huddled up in the corner. I asked him why he was there and in my mind; he told me he had died alone, nobody came, he was very lonely. I told Sue that he was pointing to me to go through a small cupboard under the stairs. Funny, I thought, but Sue said to me, "Go on then". I must have given her a funny look so I took the plunge, opened the small doorway and as I did so I found myself in another room, which was the back of the cottage part. It had stairs going up to the first floor. As I then tuned in again, somebody was calling me from a bedroom. As I approached the room, it made me jump, there was a woman in white in the corner crying. She told me she was looking for her children. She had a Scottish accent, she also said she was hiding because her dad was looking for her and she was scared. I had to tell this lady she was now in the next world, her loved ones are there waiting for her. She can now move on from this room as she is free, I said some prayers and then she went into the light. The story was that years ago, people, mainly women, would come to Pakefield from Scotland sometimes in boats to work on the beach, sorting out the fish and gutting them. This was the catch from the night before that the fisherman brought in and they used to get paid for it. I think that Sue's house in the past was used for the workers to stay in while they did that work. I do think that the lady in white passed away at an early age leaving two children to fend for themselves.

Sue then asked me if I could go into the front bedroom, as she had seen people walking through in the night. I went in and as I did so my guide, Ralfeta, warned me to be careful because apparently, the front of the house where they had built on was on a ley line, this is a pathway that was there years ago, it leads from the Pakefield church to the pub on the hill (this is why I kept getting this feeling with the church) smugglers used it as it was underground and not seen by the authorities in times gone by. As we went downstairs, Sue told me about a parrot she had in a cage that was sick. Then I realised it was on the ley line and told her to move the cage off and she let me know later that the parrot recovered.

I actually a little while after, went to the churchyard to have a look at the gravestones and noticed there were people buried there who were pirates from long ago, of course, then in my head, I heard someone call me as I looked around I was drawn to a grave, I knew his name was John before I looked I realised I was looking at the organist that played the organ for seven years, he said he was looking for Anne his wife. I said a prayer for him in my mind hoping this would be enough so he could find Anne in spirit.

Chapter Six

Our Pets

I write this chapter with a broken heart, as we have just lost our beloved boxer dog, Daisy. I know she was with us for nearly thirteen years, which is a good age for that type of dog. As I am writing this, I am sure so many of you out there have been through the same emotions of losing a well-loved pet, actually I feel for every single person who goes through it, be it on the TV or someone telling me. Loads of people over the years have asked do our pets go into the spirit world. The answer to that question is yes. Yes, I have done many readings in the past where a special pet comes in, it's usually with a special loved one who is now in spirit, they come just to let their family know that they are alright and the pet has come home. I always make sure I console that person by being able to see their pet and it helps the sitter a lot. We have to grieve like we would a family member or friend because that is what they are, but really the hurt is real. I would like to share with you what I wrote after her passing, it helps to write it all down.

Daisy's Story from Her Point of View

One day we, as puppies, were playing and getting up to mischief, having a scrap, once I even wet the carpet or the odd mess when I missed the newspaper, put down for us puppies. Still, they won't know it was me, as there are seven of us. Then there was a ring on the doorbell and strangers came and took my siblings away one by one until there was just me left, you see I am white, nobody wants a white one, no good for breeding I heard them say, until one day a kind lady came along with her daughter by the name of Kelly. She loved me being white, no problem there, I heard them say. Kelly loved me, we walked, we played, she cuddled me, I was happy again.

The happiness was short-lived though, they called me Daisy because Kelly's mum saw a field of daisies and decided I looked like them, anyway let's play again Kelly but she was crying, I have to go away, cannot stay here, no dogs in the flat where we lived, that must be me. A friend took me away to be with her family, a house filled with children. Lovely, so I thought, only I am cold and hungry and shut out of the house all the time. You see, us boxers do not have a lot of fur to keep us warm, I am unhappy my tail is gone between my legs. (This was the first four months of Daisy's life)

Then on the 25 of February, we gave her a home, Daisy did go through a lot in her life both her back legs were operated on as the cruciate ligaments had gone in both of her knees and in later years she had an operation after operation as she had a lot of lumps removed but she survived nearly thirteen years, cost us a lot of money but she was worth it, I always said there were three in this marriage now after her passing it is two of us again.

I advise anybody going through the same thing to write about it and bring their special qualities to pen and paper. Remember the good times and the bad will disappear. We are now in 2013, the world is becoming a war zone. It is harder for me to accept all this bombing and killing simply because I keep asking for peace for the world, it's just not happening. I do think though, one day it will come but with a price tag attached to it, it was at this time, when we were sitting in a circle that I had an out-of-body experience and what came through was worrying as I was told that in 2030 something was going to happen to turn the world upside down and a lot of people were going to die. As I thought about it after and the helpers in the circle discussed it, we thought perhaps there might be another war or the weather may play a big part in it but we had to leave it there because there were more questions than answers. For the next three years, I carried on with my job and also the readings kept coming but in a way, I think spirit worked it out and they pressured me into retirement.

On my last Christmas, at home in 2016, I was going to leave but the other cook that worked with me on the other shift became very ill and she had to have a few months off in the meantime, the boss got another cook to do my hours and I stayed till the May of that year. After I retired, we decided to get another puppy. We called her, Rosie, she is a Staffordshire bull terrier and now I am at home with her and making a decision to start thinking about writing this book. I could never have thought about having another dog after Daisy but time heals and when you are a dog lover life is not the same without a dog. Rosie is a darling but a handful, she also gets me walking which is a good thing.

Many people still phone me for readings as the spirit will always want me to work for them, which I understand there may come a time when I cannot be there for my people but now I have time and I enjoy it. Sometimes the spirit approaches me when I least expect it, I can go into an area may be the shops or a coffee shop and I feel spirit around me.

Just recently, I have been given a set of cards, I have always said that they are a prop not something you need but I found it helps a lot to bring something to life that is not always in the reading it just needs the courage to trust what you are being given, also John and I went to the Isle of Wight for a holiday and while we were there, we found a lovely shop with crystals, some felt very special so I bought them and now using them in my readings, gives something special to the person who I am reading for. Talking about that now brings a time when more and more people are going online, which is the way forward. Talking to Sarah my daughter-in-law, she knows more than me about websites, etc. as I do not have much idea when it comes to the web but we will be planning something in the future as this is a way forward as her Belle, my granddaughter, is eleven now Sarah has more time on her hands, so watch out for that.

Now we have approached 2020 I guess you will know what I am about to talk about, the lockdown, this virus which has turned us all upside down this is what I saw back in 2016 problem was, when I was given this information and saw the date I was given in my mind, which was 2030 but it looks like I got it wrong as I saw lots of people dying and the world turned upside down on its axis is what I was told and I think it is this virus, I was being shown as the whole world has been turned upside down. I have decided to write this book out properly from rough notes that I kept over the years in lockdown number two and three and hope that I have now helped a lot of people understand a lot more about what can be achieved in life when we follow our hearts.

Chapter Seven

Epilogue of My Life

If I had to, I would live my life again knowing what I know now, happiness. From that small girl losing her mother at the age of six, being taken away from her father and older sister, Pauline, and then being put into care. First by a foster family, where the man abused me and I was scared to say anything, my sister May was with me. From there, we were taken away from these abusers to where we spent a lovely year with our Granny Harmer in Horam Sussex. Sadly, it was only a year of happiness as my father remarried; she was the stepmother from hell, she locked us both out of the house all day so when we were not at school, we had to roam the streets. I always felt hungry, it always seemed to rain a lot then so we had to go to the bus shelters to keep dry, other children from the school used to call us names. When it was nighttime, no television or anything like that. I remember me and my sister were locked in the attic, there we had a bed only no toys and you could see the rafters and a bolt was put across so we could not get out. This went on for a long time. Then one day, my sister Pauline came looking for us and, of course, we were not at home. She apparently then went next door to ask about us and the neighbours told her what had been going on. Pauline did no more but reported it to the social authorities and action was taken from there, our awful stepmother had a go at us before we were taken away that we did not say goodbye to our father but now when I think about it, it upset me at the time it did work both ways. He could have seen us off on the day but he was nowhere to be seen, must have gone to work. My sister and I were taken to a children's home in Waterlooville, Portsmouth. I believe now it saved us both from ourselves, although I still went through a lot up until the age of forty but there was a reason for that. My guide has told me that to become a good medium, you have either suffered in life you have been given, or illness overtakes you while you are on this earth, usually, we only use a small part of the brain while we are living, if you go through illness or trauma it fills up the part that is needed while we are here if that happens, we spill over into our soul, the part, that is used when we pass over, this is how and why we can communicate with the spirit world.

I know I have my sister Pauline to thank for all that she did for us, she saved us, I have to say this whole heartily as she passed away suddenly in 2018 and I owe so much to her, so to finish my story, I need to say thank you and I love you. Just to say, always tell your loved ones how you feel about them because one day you cannot. I am a medium but I do not always get the answers.